THE Ratel SAGA

Ratel

MELLIVORA CAPENSIS

Published by Sanderley Studios

Story Copyright 2022 by Lawdog

Illustrations Copyright 2022 by Cedar Sanderson

www.sanderleystudios.com

One year in Nigeria, Chris and I discovered the books of Gerald Durrell, and the wonderful world contained therein.

It didn't take long for the two of us to decide that Mr. Durrell probably needed assistance in his acquisition of animals for his zoo, so we decided to capture local species and send them to him.

Before I go any further, I should inform the Gentle Reader that at the time this took place, the national sport of Nigeria seemed to be revolution.

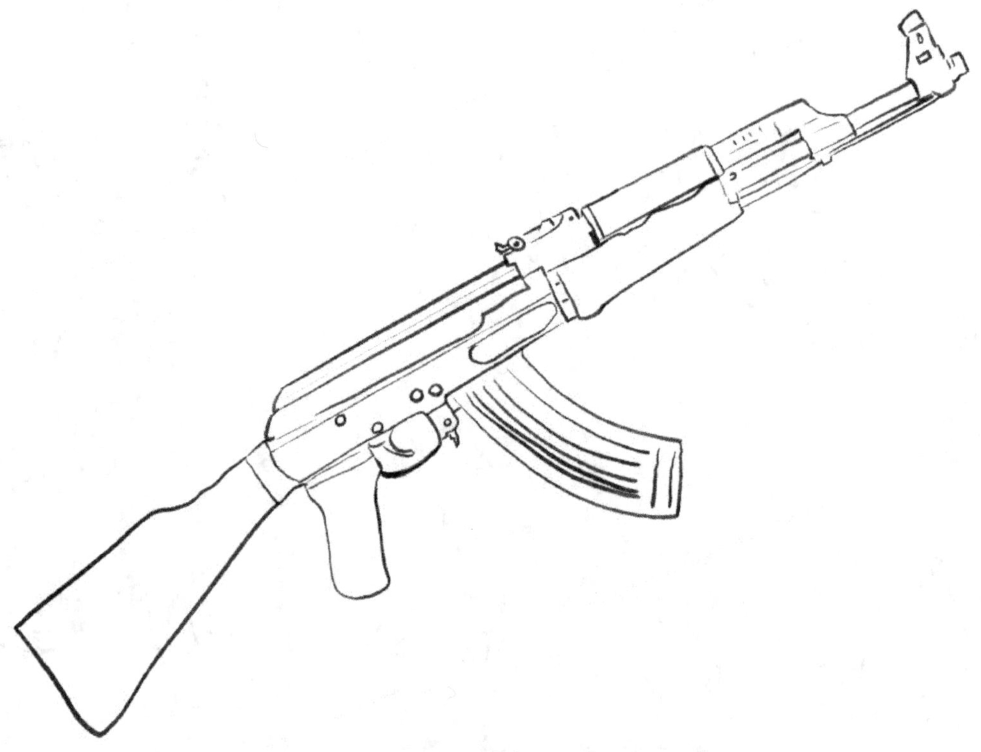

Anyhoo, after several days of chasing things through jungle and swamp, Mom had decided that the active route to animal capture was a bit too ... strenuous:

Mom (slightly big-eyed, and stiff): "Is that a green mamba in that jar?"

Dad (tapping on jar with forefinger): "I don't think so. Looks like a green vine snake. Harmless."

Mom: "Thank God."

Kids: "Are you sure it's not a mamba?"

Dad: "Yes. Small gripping teeth only. No fangs."

Kids (with feeling): "Bugger!"

Philothamnus
semivariegatus
Dendroaspis
angusticeps

Confined to the back-yard it didn't take too long for us to realize that sneaking up on animals was a wee bit difficult if every animal within nine square miles is actively avoiding getting anywhere near our back-yard.

I have suspicions that the surviving astro-lizards had been spreading malicious propaganda regarding our activities, but however word spread we couldn't find anything bigger than a bug in the yard.

After much pondering on the extensive cowardice of the daylight species, we decided to see if the lack of moral fiber extended to the nocturnal varieties. Since Mom would never allow us to lurk in the back-yard until dawn, obviously we needed to build a trap of some kind.

Out came the shovels.

As a point of pride I would like to inform the Gentle Reader that -- by God! -- Chris and I dug that hole down shoulder-deep before the gardener came out, contemplated our engineering thus far, shrugged, grabbed his shovel and laid to with a will. Shortly to be joined by the estate gardener, whom, upon seeing his compatriot excavating, apparently figured, "Mine not to reason why," grabbed his shovel and 'round about twilight we had one heck of a tiger pit. Required ladders for the grown-ups to get out.

Beautemous.

Dad, of course, was brought out to inspect the work of his progeny. He made the proper parental noises, then mentioned, absent-mindedly, that as narrow as the pit was, bigger species might be able to scramble out. The traditional solution, he went on to say, was to place stakes near the top of the pit angled down.

Stunned by the simplicity and beauty of this, we immediately chopped some bamboo stakes and added them to the pit.

So. Before we go any further, I wish the Gentle Reader to fix firmly in his, or her, mind a pit. Measuring about six feet long, by about six feet wide. Eight to ten feet deep. At the top of which are not one, but two rows of downward angled bamboo stakes. Which, given the nature of bamboo, are wickedly sharp.

Call it a double-wide grave from hell.

Across the top of this, picture two misanthropic little hellions happily spreading a thick layer of palm leaves and a little dirt, for realism.

Yeah.

Next morning, Chris and I go sprinting out to our trap to discover what the night had wrought. And -- oh joyous day! -- the palm fronds which had been laid to disguise the trap had been disturbed. Matter-of-fact, most of them were gone. This boded quite well, and (quivering with excitement) we snuck up on the trap to discover ...

...a **RATEL.**

For those in the audience who are
not familiar with African fauna, 'ratel' is an
Afrikaans word meaning 'Psychopathic
Buzzsaw From Hell'.

Also called a 'honey badger', a ratel is
best described as 500 pounds of pure
distilled pissed-off crammed into a 25
pound body.

To get a proper perspective,
understand that wildebeasts and buffalo
have been found dead after a ratel attack,
and that lions and hyenas will give an
irritated ratel a wide berth.

And we had one of the little darlings in our trap. The day was looking good.

Now, the ratel at the bottom of our pit wasn't a fully-grown member of the
species. Matter-of-fact, looking back, I'm pretty sure he was a bit more sullen than
other ratels we had run across, and might have had a bit of a sneer, so he was most
probably a teenage ratel.

Anyhoo, Chris and I had concocted a complicated plot to extract our ratel using
a banana tree trunk, four innertubes, a chicken and a peanut sack, when Brigadier-
Captain Azikiwe showed up.

sigh

Brigadier-Captain Azikiwe was one of those annoying little gits who constantly
has a finger up, testing the breeze. No matter who was in power, Azikiwe had always
been one of his most loyal subjects. In other words, he was a complete toady, lick-
spittle and yes-man. The only convictions he had ever carried were in his criminal
record. Thoroughly irritating little suck-up.

In addition to his other charming attributes, Azikiwe was a bit of a bully. Since
he was alarmingly small, the only safe targets were those smaller than him.

Which would normally include Chris and myself, unfortunately, 1) We were the
offspring of Chief Jim, the Big Boss of the Plant, major source of bribes for a
struggling Nigerian Army Officer/Civilian Junior Minister of Gummint (depending on
who was in power that month); and 2) We really didn't give a damn.

Which, near as I can tell, was the reason that Azikiwe barely tolerated us.

Mom, on the other paw, asserts that the Brigadier-Captain actively loathed us,
and was entirely due to the Famous Phydeaux Lunch Incident.

Phydeaux was our Yard Frog. He was also a West African Giant Frog, which meant he was about the size of a small terrier. He lived under a rock in one of the flower beds and was responsible for outside varmint control.

On the Lunch Incident Day, Phydeaux had decided to nosh on a juvenile Ball Python, who held opinions most firm about the matter. The debate wound up under the house, which was a decided no-no for Phydeaux, due to his habit of singing the froggy version of "Henry the Eighth, I am, I am" in the wee hours of the morning, and when under the house, directly under Mom's pillow.

So, to prevent the execution of the stated promise of "Frog Jambalaya", Chris and I scooted under the house to extract Phydeaux.

PYXICEPHALUS ADSPERSUS

Now, you may not know that Ball Pythons get their name from their habit of rolling up into a tight ball to avoid predators. Junior had done this exact thing, and was fortunate in that as big as Phydeaux was, the balled-up python was just a wee smidgen bigger than Phydeaux could get into his maw.

We got there as the frustrated frog was rolling the snake about, trying to get a thumb into the coils to unwind the munchie, to no avail. We separated snake and frog, causing Phydeaux to retreat under a beam to sulk.

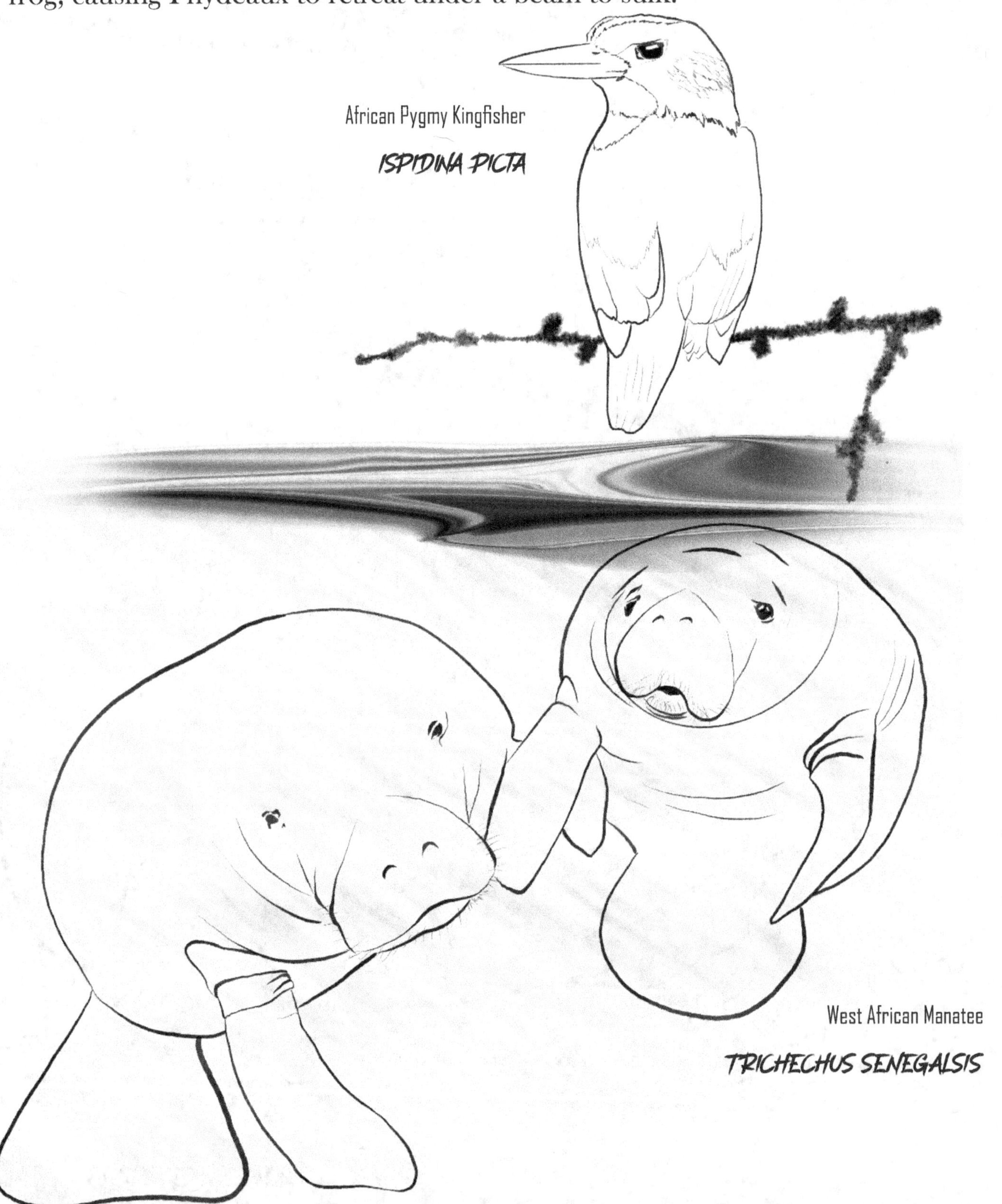

African Pygmy Kingfisher

ISPIDINA PICTA

West African Manatee

TRICHECHUS SENEGALSIS

Hoping to take Phydeaux's one-track little amphibian mind off of lunch, Chris grabbed the snake and backed out from under the house. And there, standing proud in the garden decked out in a crisp khaki uniform absolutely dripping with yards of gilt, was Brigadier-Captain Azikiwe, come to pay his respects and hint gently that he was more than happy to give any orphaned bribe money a good home.

Chris, seeing a handy adult, and not wanting to waste a perfectly good snake, promptly grabbed the paw that Azikiwe had regally extended, dumped the snake into it, said, "Hold this!", slapped Azikiwe's other paw onto the top of the snake-ball and dove back under the house.

scratch, scratch

You know, the last thing one would expect to find in a West Africa native is a snake phobia.

Unexpected, really.

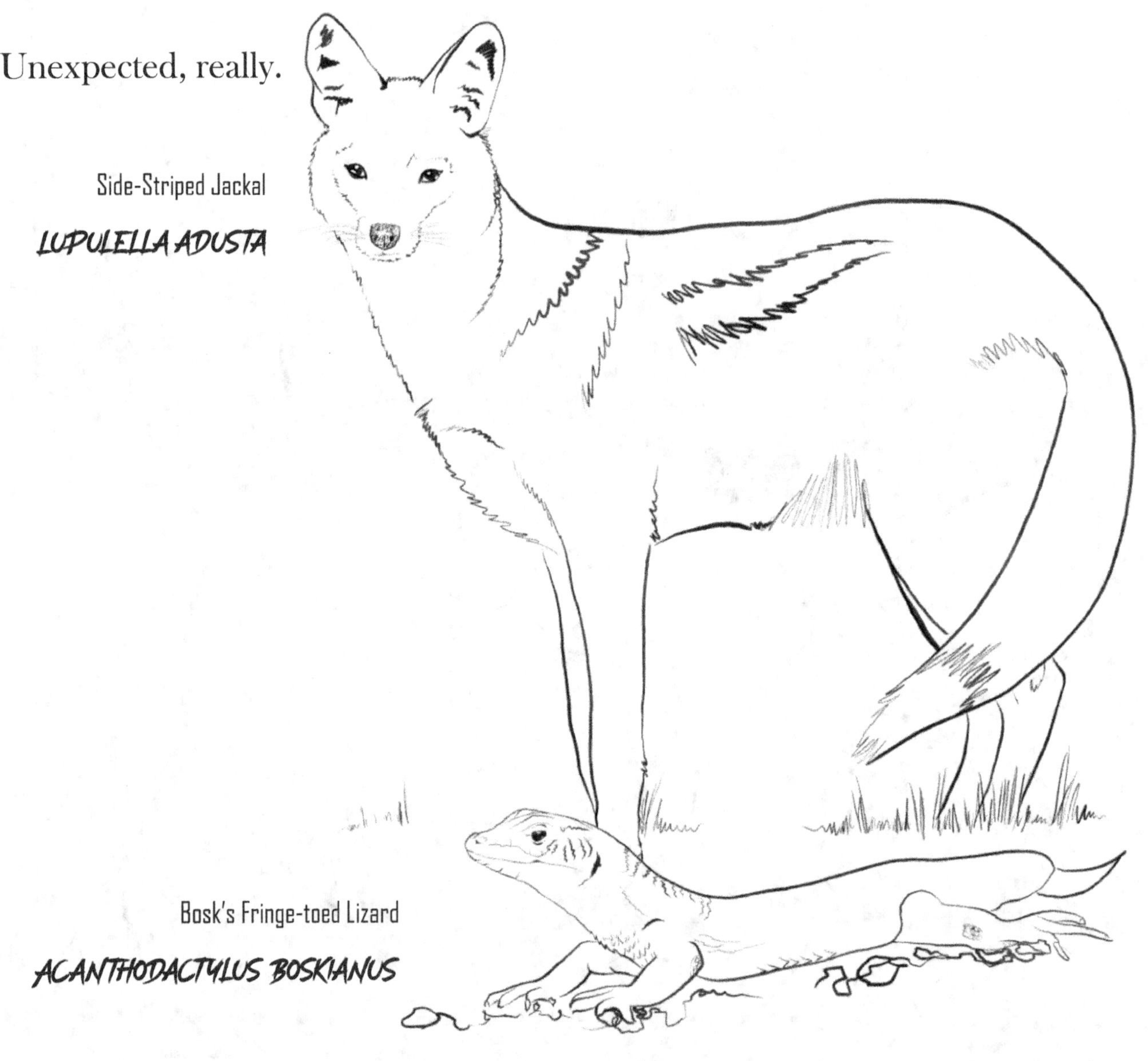

Side-Striped Jackal

LUPULELLA ADUSTA

Bosk's Fringe-toed Lizard

ACANTHODACTYLUS BOSKIANUS

Anyhoo, Chris and I managed to coax the sulking Phydeaux out from under the house, only to discover that the person to whom Chris had entrusted the snake had apparently decided to take a nap, face-first, right on our lawn.

This, in and of itself, was nothing surprising. Several of Mom and Dad's friends had been found in an identical state on Saturday mornings, although they were usually on the carpet, so we really didn't think too much of it.

We did, however, want our snake back. After lifting and checking various limbs and pockets, and rolling the unconscious Brigadier-Captain over, it became apparent that the snake either wasn't present on the carcass, or that the Azikiwe had hidden it somewhere even we couldn't find.

Getting a bit frustrated, Chris poked and prodded the Brigadier-Captain into semi-consciousness and immediately demanded, "Oy! What about our snake, then?"

Brigadier-Captain Azikiwe stared at us for a moment, and then looked at Chris, shrieked like a girl and dashed pell-mell for the street.

Good riddance, I say. Although we never did discover what the hell he did with our snake, the bastard.

Anyhoo, back to the current story. We have a ratel in a pit. We have Brigadier-Captain Azikiwe in all his smarmy glory. Can it get any better?

Flat African Dung Beetle

ONTHOPHAGUS DEPRESSUS

Okay, we've got a ratel in a pit, me and my brother with a banana-tree-trunk, four innertubes, a chicken and a peanut sack; and Brigadier-Captain Azikiwe.

Oh, and Azikiwe's two bodyguards.

Before I go any further, I want it noted for the record that Chris and I had nothing to do with Azikiwe getting bodyguards. That was Not Our Fault. We were Innocent Bystanders on that one.

sigh

Right after we discovered the wonder of Ammonium Tri-iodide -- which led to the unfortunate incident with the back-door-steps (Word to the Wise: Sapper lizards. Good theory; bad practice) -- which led to the permanent, and mysterious, disappearance of our chemistry sets, one of Dad's engineer buddies gave us a book on medieval siege weaponry.

Immediately and thoroughly fascinated by the subject, Chris and I constructed a trebuchet out of 2 X 4 timbers and a bucket of concrete which flung croquet balls an impressive distance, for all that it stood about four feet tall.

Our efforts and subsequent activities were watched with great interest by the horde of not-quite-drunk-yet engineers who were more-or-less permanently encamped at our house.

Whom, once Chris and I decided to upgrade our trebuchet, began to give us advice. And maybe some guidance. A little oversight. And a lent paw here-and-there.

Of course, they wound up taking over.

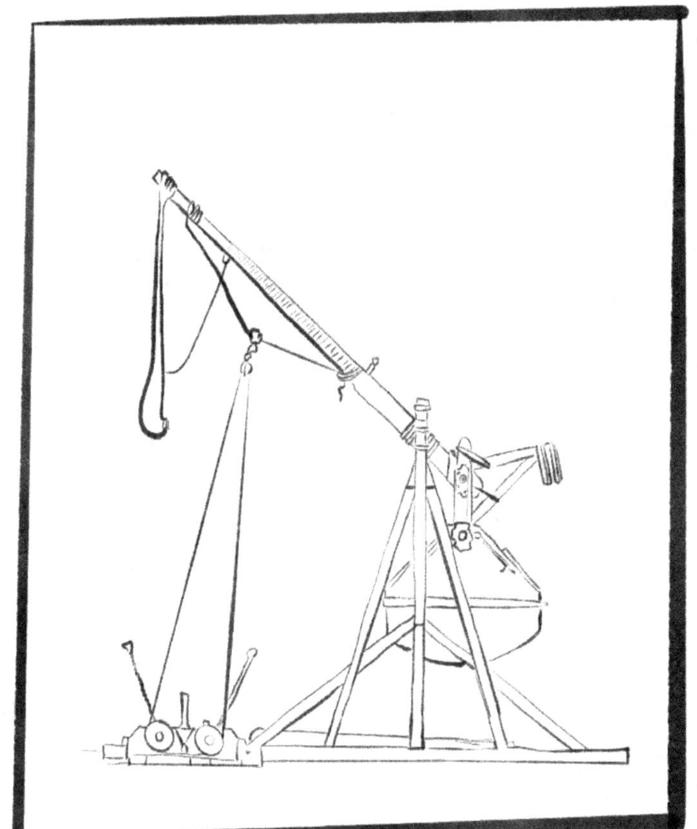

Not that we minded so much -- especially after someone fired up the arc welder.

The results were absolutely beautemous. The counterweight was drill pipe. A lot of drill pipe. The business arm was almost up to the house eaves when unloaded. Needed a winch truck to drag it into firing position.

Like I said: beautemous.

Once complete, Mom, being less-intoxicated than the rest of the bunch (note that I did not say 'sober'), drove us the hundred yards to the scrap-field behind the office, where us kids helped the adults stack a bunch of empty 55-gallon drums three deep as a simulated castle wall so that we'd have a proper target for our Engine of Doom, and Mom hung a suitably defiant tablecloth as a flag for the rebellious defenders.

Then ... the Moment of Truth. Dad fetched his 16-pound bowling ball from the closet. Mom ceremoniously poured a beer over it, before it was loaded into the sling, and after a respectful pause, Dad's Brit Buddy whacked the firing pin with a sledge-hammer.

The result was ... magnificent. I never saw the arm move. One moment it was down, the next moment it was vertical. And the sound. A mighty crash it was.

"Did it go?"

"Oh, hell, yes."

"I told you [hic] the release hook needed more hook."

"'S'going, [gurgle] innit?"

"Aye, but maybe more..." a finger pointed somewhat horizontally, "...'n' less..." the finger pointed more-or-less vertically.

"Dear," said Dad, somewhat bemusedly, "Did we bring the range rover back?"

Mom waved the keys at him.

"Oh," sloshed a Brit engineer, "'Oo the hell is that [hic] then?"

"Isn't that that little [hiccup] sticky-fingered chappie with uniform? Sneezy?"

"Azikiwe?"

"Geshundheit."

Sure enough, down there in the middle of the company scrap-field -- having had to open a couple of gates to get there, I might add -- was Brigadier-Captain Azikiwe. And his Nigerian-Army-Issue Land Cruiser. Which was parked about twenty feet away from the wall of Barrel Castle, where Azikiwe was ...

"Is he **STEALING MY TABLECLOTH?!**"

Sure enough. Apparently, after having successfully infiltrated private land, and a gate, and then company land, and another gate, Azikiwe had spotted a perfectly good tablecloth hanging on some barrels and had decided -- out of the kindness of his heart, you understand -- to give this abandoned tablecloth a loving home. And had clambered to the top of Barrel Castle wall in his philanthropic endeavour.

"Oh, hard luck, old girl."

"He can't ... I didn't ... That little ... How DARE ..."

About that time, Azikiwe's Nigerian-Army-Issue Land Cruiser suddenly kind of bottomed-out. And the window glass kind of sprayed across the scrap-yard, along with the roof sort of crumpling up, followed by this wonderfully baritone CRUMP sound.

"Cor..." opined the witnesses. Glass clinked off glass, and then off teeth. There was a Contemplative Moment.

"A skosh [hic] right, I think."

"Nah, a bit more [gurgle] than a skosh, I'd say."

"Izzat a military term [hic] ?"

"And more hook to the hook."

"RELOAD!"

Chris and I hared off to the scrap-yard to retrieve our bowling ball ordnance, which turned out to not be very difficult, since the drivers side door of the Land Cruiser (One ea., Nigerian Army Issue) was laying in the dirt.

We had just pried the bowling ball out of the drivers seat, and were scooting back to the trebuchet when one of the palm trees lining the fence of the scrap yard said, and I quote: "PidginpidginpidginDEVIL CHILDRENpidginpidgin!"

Sure enough, peering from the top of the palm tree was the Brigadier-Captain. Looked damned odd without his aviator glasses and corn-cob pipe, and the ashy sheen to his face clashed terribly with the gilt on the uniform, but it was definitely him.

"PidginpidginBAD JUJUpidginpidgin!"

Figuring that this was one of those Adult Situations Mom and Dad had told us about, we returned to the house, the palm tree still shrieking curses at us.

"He still there?"

"He's in one of the palm trees over by the right-hand gate."

"Not for long he's bloody well not," giggled an engineer as he lovingly placed a wicker laundry hamper full of empty beer cans on the sling.

Which doesn't sound altogether too bad, until you realize that beer cans back then were made out of steel.

Didn't even come close to Azikiwe, but the racket of the ensuing multiple impacts in the general neighborhood caused the Brigadier-Captain to retreat under fire, as it were, legging it down the road to safety, and leaving his issue Land Cruiser as a war trophy, repatriated back to the Nigerian Army only after six weeks of negotiations and conditions.

And somehow, he wound up blaming Chris and me for this.

I don't know what he was whinging about, anyway. He got bodyguards out of it, didn't he?

Anyhoo, there we were. Ratel. Pit. Bodyguards.

I hate it when things don't act the way they're supposed to. For instance, an animal which has found itself at the bottom of an eight-foot pit is supposed to pace about, dig, fidget, maybe jump at the walls a bit. They're not supposed to sit at the bottom of the pit and look up at you, batting their eyelashes and looking all cute and cuddley.

Chris and I knew cute-and-cuddley. Hell, we had Ph.D's in the art of looking cute-and-cuddley -- usually prior-to, during, or just after all Damnation breaking loose -- so we weren't exactly fooled by the facade. The only thing we weren't sure of, was how much bluff was hiding behind the Great Big Puppy Eyes Look.

A situation requiring much delicacy, and maybe some planning, all of which went out the window when Azikiwe walked up.

He casually glanced into our pit, did a double-take, then motioned to his body-guards, who sullenly stepped up, before doing double-takes of their own.

I knew the little bastard was up to no good when he turned to us with that huge grin, and said, "Oh, na picken, dis beef very, very bad. Too much bad for you" and took out his dress pistol.

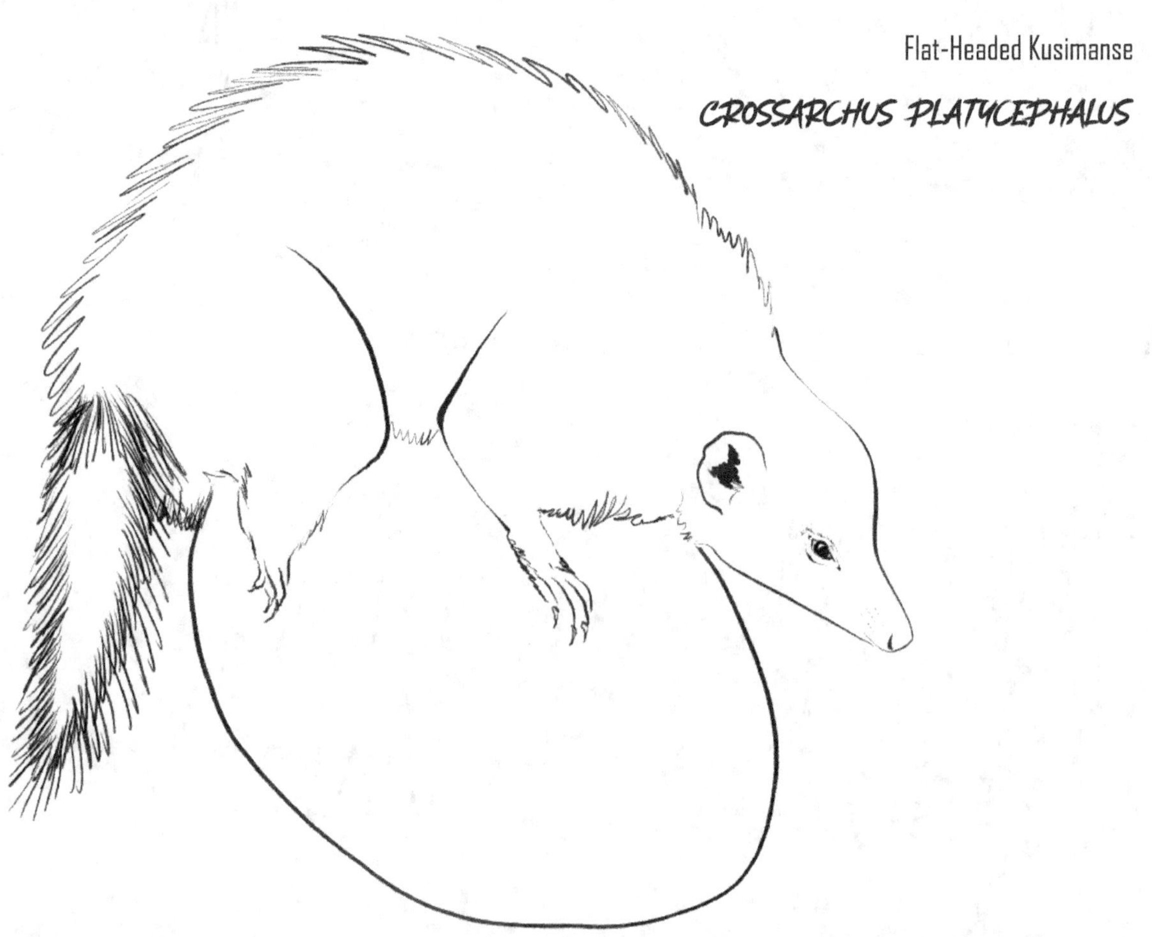

Flat-Headed Kusimanse

CROSSARCHUS PLATYCEPHALUS

He jacked the slide on what I dimly recall as maybe something Italian in the 6.35 or 7.65 millimetre range, sighted on the ratel in the pit, and stepped to one side for a better angle ...

... trodding firmly upon the chicken we had fetched as part of our Ratel Extraction Kit ...

... who took this as a grave insult, and promptly jumped into Azikiwe's face, wings flapping, talons up, and cussing a blue streak in Poultry ...

... a full-on beserker attack from a rooster is enough to startle anyone, much less Brigadier-Captain Azikiwe, who cannot be blamed for taking a startled leap backwards ...

... however, it was **NOT OUR FAULT** that a bodyguard was standing in Azikiwe's plotted touchdown point, said impact causing Azikiwe to ricochet somewhat less than gracefully off the bodyguard ...

... before vanishing in the shadowed depths of our ratel trap.

You know, there is a peaceful, almost serene, moment that occurs just after the last chance to prevent the fit from hitting the shan, a moment that is almost like a deep sigh as if the Universe is thinking about what a nice day it had been up to that point, and in all that quiet, you can quite clearly hear that little voice in the back of your head saying: "Oh, bugger."

And then the shrieking and bellowing started.

Down in the pit, Azikiwe was doing a full-on sprint, in reverse. In one hand he held one of our bamboo stakes, which he was using to frantically swat at the ratel, who was likewise at a full sprint. Only, not in reverse.

To this day, I have no idea what happened to the pistol. I suspect that somebody down in the hole ate it, although I'm not quite sure whom.

It was fairly obvious that either Azikiwe or the ratel needed out of the hole. Seeing as how Azikiwe had opposable thumbs, he was the logical choice, so I grabbed up the nearest rope-like item that we had brought to the trap, laid down next to the hole and put the free end over the side for the Brigadier-Captain to grab and hopefully pull himself out.

In case the question ever arises, an innertube from a bicycle tire is not the best choice for this kind of thing, trust me on this one.

Azikiwe got a firm grip, one might even go so far as to say a death-grip, on the innertube, and pulled down as he jumped.

The innertube, being rubber, promptly sttttrrrreeeeccchhhhed and maybe didn't give the Brigadier-Captain as much boost as he might have expected. Or wanted.

He managed to hook his chin over the lip of the pit, and began furiously pedaling his feet against the walls. Which produced absolutely no lift. He then began frantically scrabbling at the grass and dirt scattered around the pit with his free arm, while still furiously pedaling his feet, and pulling firmly on the rubber tube -- all of these actions combined not doing much more than producing a slow slide back into the pit.

Chris, in the meantime, was rolling the banana tree trunk to the pit. Since the trunk was a good bit longer than the pit was wide, when he got it positioned across the pit there was about a two foot overlap on either end.

He then ran around to one end of the trunk and began to push it into the trap, hopefully producing a ramp out of the hole for whomever decided to use it first.

I began calculating the distance to the nearest palm tree.

And Azikiwe hit bottom.

There was a happy, almost joyous, scream from the honey-badger, followed by a most unhappy shriek from Azikiwe and then Azikiwe came out of the trap like he had a furry JATO bottle attached to his butt and clamped both arms onto the middle of the banana tree trunk, followed by both legs.

This was a Bad Thing. Since Chris didn't have the trunk pushed into the trap yet, the Brigadier-Captain wound up dangling from the trunk. With twelve pounds of pissed-off ratel dangling from Azikiwe.

With the added weight, the combined push power of both myself and Chris wasn't up to getting the trunk into the hole. And since the ratel not only had a firm grip on one cheek, he also had the claws of one paw firmly hooked into Azikiwe's Sam Browne belt, he wasn't coming loose until he was damned good and ready. His extra weight meant that the Brigadier-Captain couldn't swing himself around to the top side of the trunk and get out that way.

Worse yet, a banana tree trunk isn't really a trunk. It's actually tightly bundled leaves packed in a sticky sap. Looks a lot like a solid tube of packed corrugated cardboard, come to think.

Anyhoo, it wasn't up to the lateral stresses of supporting the weight of both Azikiwe and the ratel and was developing a slight, though alarming, bend.

Chris told Azikiwe that he needed to turn loose of the trunk, so that we could get it into the hole and he could scramble out.

Azikiwe didn't seem to see the logic. And, you know, I'm no-where near being a prude, but I wouldn't have couched my reply in the language Azikiwe used, not around kids, anyway.

Thinking that maybe if the honey-badger turned loose, Azikiwe would be able to scramble around the trunk to safety, I snatched up the chicken (who had hung around to see What Happened Next) by the legs and (leaning precariously out over the pit I might add) waved it next to the ratel's head, hoping to tempt into letting go.

Apparently, ratels are firm believers in the old maxim "A Bird In The Hand Is Worth Two In The Bush" -- or in this case "A Ham In The Jaws Is Worth Any Number Of Free Range Chickens" -- 'cause he showed not one sign of turning loose.

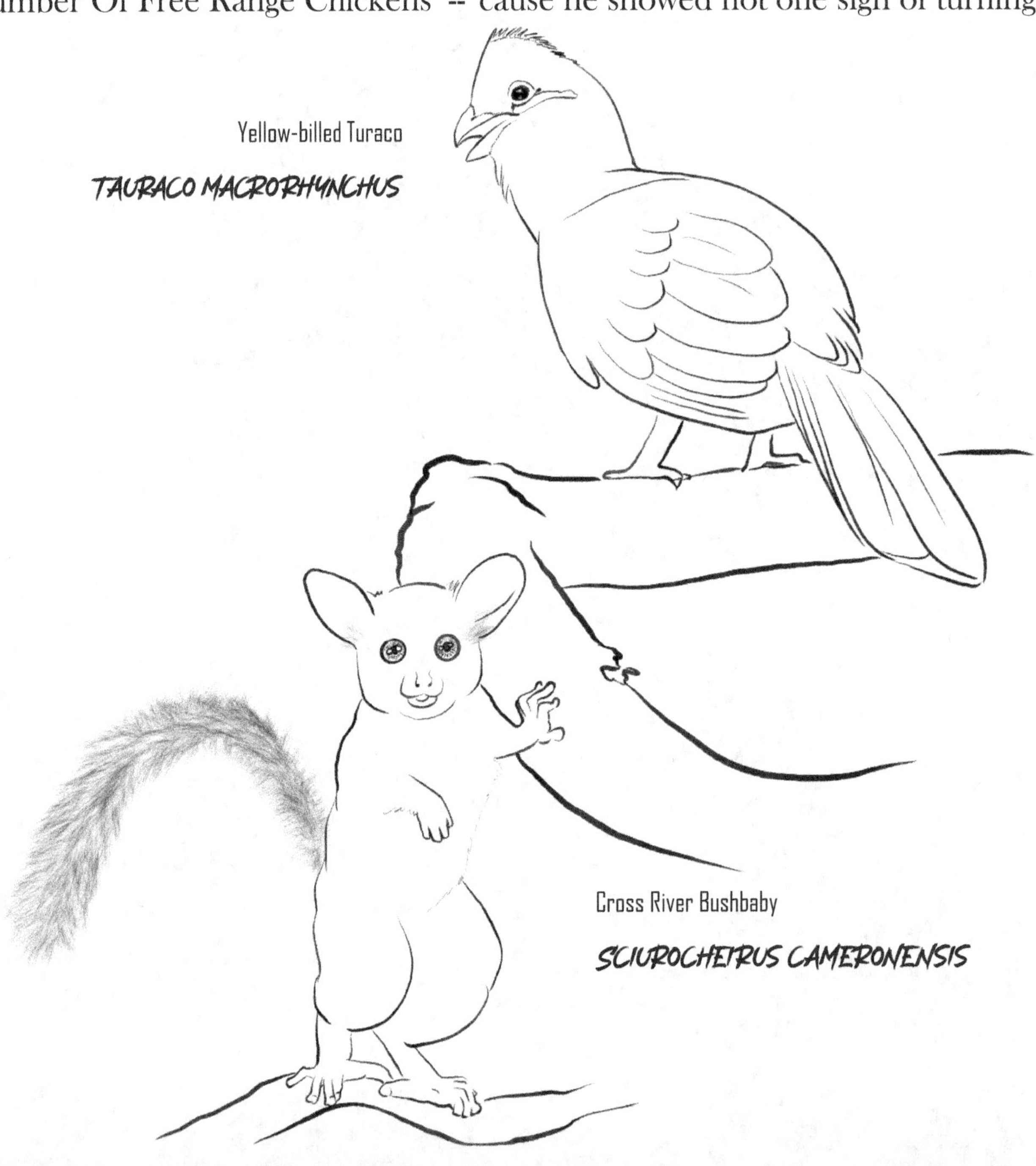

Yellow-billed Turaco

TAURACO MACRORHYNCHUS

Cross River Bushbaby

SCIUROCHEIRUS CAMERONENSIS

The rooster, on the other paw, held Certain Views vis a vis Being Volunteered for Dinner Detail, and promptly came unwound.

Not being entirely gormless, however, the chicken was more than happy to deliver the pecks and wing-strikes to Azikiwe, rather than the twelve-pound berserk carnivore trying to get his other paw latched onto todays meal.

Azikiwe's response to my bit of aid would have had Old School, salty, tar-and-teak sailors saying, "Steady on, that's going a bit far, that is."

And then trunk bent a little more.

You know, a man -- or boy -- has got to know his limits.

"DAA-AAD!!"

Red-billed Oxpecker

BUPHAGUS ERYTHRORYNCHUS

Warthog

PHACOCHOERUS AFRICANUS

It was my parents custom on Saturday mornings to have a late breakfast on the patio, while leisurely perusing a copy of the London Gazette or the London Daily Telegraph, whichever newspaper was less than two weeks old.

They were usually joined by Dad's Brit Buddy, Tom, and whoever had survived the previous evening.

The following conversation has been pieced together from various witnesses to the incident. I make no guarantees as to the accuracy.

Tom: "Your children just ran past me carrying a burlap sack and a chicken."

Dad (from behind the paper): "They dug a tiger pit in the backyard yesterday. Probably got another snake or something."

Tom: "Oh, well, then. Ta, luv."

Mom (pouring tea): "How deep did they dig?"

Dad (feeling around for his coffee cup): "Mmm. Probably borrowed a Chinese coolie or two for the last hundred feet."

Tom: "Oh, what rotten luck."

Mom (shading her eyes): "If that's Azikiwe, you owe me five pounds."

Tom: "Just because Sticky-fingers is here, it doesn't necessarily follow that the raft didn't sink. And when did he start having an escort?"

Mom (moving Dad's coffee cup under his hand): "The boys dropped a bowling ball on his car."

Tom: "I missed that? Where was I for that? Oh. I say, one of Sneezy's guards just tossed the poor blighter into the hole."

Mom: "They obviously know him."

Dad's newspaper: "Mmm."

Mom: "Scone?"

Tom: "Thank you. Did your children sign a truce with Sneezy? Looks like they're trying to get him out. Jolly good show, that."

Mom: "Did that soldier just swat the other soldier on the back of the head?"

Appreciative sips from cups.

Tom: "Nice cursing match. Do either of you understand a word they're saying?"

Dad: (turning page) "Mothers. Goats. Unusual sexual practices ..."

Tom: "Oh, nice shove, that."

Dad: "... Stupidity. Improbable ancestry. The usual."

Tom: "And a nice kick to the shins, there. Classic. Any milk, luv?"

Mom: "I am NOT breaking up a fight between two soldiers. What is my child doing?"

Long pause.

Tom: "Jim."

Dad: "Mmm?"

Tom: "One of your children is bludgeoning Brigadier-Captain Azikiwe with a chicken."

Mom: "Truce must be off. That soldier shoves the other one any harder and there's going to be two of them in the hole."

Dad (absent-mindedly) "Which chicken?"

Tom: "Does it matter? You've got two soldiers rolling around in your backyard biting and smacking each other, and one of your offspring is assaulting an African army officer with that big-arsed red rooster!"

Dad (meditatively): "That's the one I'd use."

Mom: "I suppose we could get the garden hose and spray them down."

Tom: "Jim, you have a problem in your backyard."

Dad (turning the page): "The soldiers will get tired of wrassling around, they'll shake hands and make up."

Tom: "Well, okay ..."

Dad: "Azikiwe will stop doing whatever is pissing off the boys, and they'll go find something else to get into. Are the kids missing any limbs?"

Tom: "No."

Dad: "See any major bleeding?"

Tom: "Well, no."

Mom: "The milk is on your side of the paper, dear."

Dad: "Are they screaming?"

"DAA-AAD!!"

Tom (to the vacant seats formerly occupied by my parents): "As a matter-of-fact..."

What is it with mothers? They ask you if you're okay, and when you say, "Yes" they go ahead and check you anyway. A process, I might add, that is exasperating enough in private, never mind in front of two soldiers and a ratel.

"Nice badger, boys," said Dad meditatively.

"Boss," yelped Azikiwe, plaintively, "Na picken, dey go too far!" Once started, he launched into an extensive whinge about the misfortunes and evils that my brother and I were, according to him, solely responsible for.

Due to the rising volume of the screech, I have never been actually sure if the growl came from the ratel, or my mother, who had picked up a lump of dirt the size of a large coconut, and was gauging both the weight and possible trajectories involving Azikiwe's head with a professional eye, but it caused my father to raise a regal finger at Azikiwe and murmur, "I am thinking."

Azikiwe hushed and hung from his banana tree trunk, with only an occasional whine from him and happy snarl from the ratel to disturb Dad's ruminations as he ambled around the scene.

Finally he paused by the two bodyguards, who had abandoned their tussle in the dirt when my parents had arrived. "Ah, soldiers," said Dad, as if they were a mild surprise, "You are well?"

Both men jumped to their feet and whipped off snappy salutes, "Yes, sah! We are well! And yourself?"

Somewhat abstractedly, Dad replied, "Fine, fine. I need two fine soldiers. Are you two such soldiers?"

Snappy salutes again. "Sah, yes, sah!"

Dad patted each one on the back, "Good. Go with madam. Honey, I think we're going to need a wooden crate."

Mom fired a last glare at Azikiwe, dropped the dirt boulder and dusted off her hands, "Two by two by four, dear?"

"Sounds about right."

"I'll bring the range rover back here, too. Less distance."

"Good, good. Tom, go to the kitchen, look in the pantry and bring me the oldest bottle of ginger beer you can find."

"Right-o."

"All right, boys, let's see what we have here..."

In short order, we had threaded rope through slits cut in the top of the peanut sack, and with the aid of bamboo poles, had worked the sack into position just below the ratel.

Dad looked around. The ropes and poles were held by a soldier on either side of the pit; Mom and Tom were standing beside a wooden ammo crate with the lid held at ready; Chris and I were safely on top of the roof of the Range Rover; and Azikiwe and the ratel still had deathgrips on their respective items.

Dad worked a church-key under the cap of the bottle of Mom's home-brewed-ginger-beer-from-Sheol he was holding, popped the cap off and put his thumb over the top.

Sniffing reflectively, Dad shook the hell out of the bottle, then leaned forward and slipped his thumb off the lip -- directing a jet of highly-pressurized, highly-spiced ginger-beer into the face of the startled honey-badger.

You know, ratels are some of the toughest critters on Mother Natures little green dirtball, but there are some things that they just aren't prepared for.

I don't know if he was going to snort, sneeze, snap or spew, but whatever was on his mind, he wound up turning loose of Brigadier-Captain Azikiwe's left ham.

Which caused him to drop quite neatly into the burlap peanut sack, his weight drawing the sack closed just as slick as a coin purse.

Dad reached out and grabbed the top of the sack just as claws appeared through the burlap at the bottom and flipped both ratel and sack into the crate, where Mom and Tom slammed the lid down, and Mom jumped up on top of the lid for good measure while Tom worked packing straps around box and lid.

To
G Durrell

"Out of the hole, Brigadier-Captain," said Dad.

"Oh, boss. I am pained too, too much."

"Suit yourself," murmured my father, while Tom and the soldiers, under the direction of my mother, heaved the snarling, rocking crate into the back of the Range Rover.

"Boss?" said the pit.

"Tom, can you watch the kids for a bit?" asked Mom, "The tea is still fresh and the paper is only about a week old."

"Boss," stated the trap.

"Be glad to," assured Tom.

"Dad! We're going to send it to Gerald Durrell!"

Dad tapped his forehead gently with two fingers, "I forgot. Dear?"

Mom found a marker pen in the glovebox of the Range Rover, and very precisely printed:

Gerald Durrell

General Delivery

England

FRAGILE! THIS END UP!

on the side of the cursing wooden crate. Then she and Dad climbed into the truck and started the engine.

"Boss!" yelped the tiger trap.

You know, I have nagging doubts about whether she and Dad actually took the ratel to the Lagos Post Office and mailed it, or whether they drove it out into the bush and set it free. We never, ever received a thank you note from Mr. Durrell, which did seem a bit out of character for the man.

"DEVIL CHILDREN!" shrieked the pit in the voice of Brigadier-Captain Azikiwe, as we bounded off to show Tom the plans for a broom-firing ballista, and did Tom think he could get his hands on some one-inch rope?

LawDog was born on the island of Malta to American parents, who promptly raised him all over Africa and the Middle East, where the story-telling culture seems to have stuck.

He has been a soldier, an EMT, a fireman, a (very briefly) short-order cook, and the world's worst rodeo clown.

He recently retired after 26 years of law enforcement.

He (currently) lives in north Texas with a very patient lady, two very well-fed chiweenies, and way too many books.

Cedar Sanderson is an author, artist, and scientist who draws dragons far too often. She grew up in Alaska, but now lives in Texas, because size isn't everything.

She has written ten novels, a bunch of short stories, and more essays than you can shake a stick at. She has also doodled up three children's books, four coloring books, and there's more coming.

She lives with a cat (who isn't hers) a dog (who also isn't hers) and a grumpy old man (who is all hers).

Draw your own ratel here:

This camel was disqualified from the beauty contest due to the use of botox and fillers.

CAMELUS DROMEDARIUS

www.ingramcontent.com/pod-product-compliance
Lightning Source LLC
Chambersburg PA
CBHW081400160726
48000CB00010B/3422